A THEFT: MY CON MAN

Hanif Kureishi grew up in Kent and studied philosophy at King's College London. His novels include *The Buddha of Suburbia*, which won the Whitbread Prize for Best First Novel, *The Black Album*, *Intimacy* and *The Last Word*. His screenplays include *My Beautiful Laundrette*, which received an Oscar nomination for Best Screenplay, *Sammy and Rosie Get Laid* and *Le Week End*. He has also published several collections of short stories. He has been awarded the Chevalier de l'Ordre des Arts et des Lettres, the PEN/Pinter Prize and is a Commander of the Order of the British Empire. His work has been translated into thirty-six languages. He is professor of Creative Writing at Kingston University.

HANIF KUREISHI

A Theft: *My Con Man*

FABER & FABER

First published in 2014
by Faber & Faber Limited
Bloomsbury House
74–77 Great Russell Street
London WC1B 3DA

Typeset by Faber & Faber Limited
Printed in the UK by CPI Group (UK) Ltd, Croydon, CR0 4YY

A CIP record for this book
is available from the British Library

ISBN 978–0–571–32319–7

2 4 6 8 10 9 7 5 3 1

'Silent, foul spiders spin their web in the base of our brain . . .'

CHARLES BAUDELAIRE, *Les Fleurs du mal*

I met a man who fed a worm into my ear, and it lived there for more than a year, where it became comfortable and began to devour my mind and eat into my brain. Colonised and infected, I was anxious and depressed, and, at times, a shell. I staggered about like a dying man and slept as much as I could; being awake was no fun. I understood hiding, denial and the passion for ignorance.

Sense is usually the last thing that anyone wants to see, but eventually the truth presses down until you have to open your eyes. I began to hate this man, whom I had only recently met, but who had led me on, and then deceived and stolen from me. At one point, it seemed, he even pretended to be me. After doing this, he disappeared but rang every day for months, with apologies, offers of help and mad promises.

[1]

I found my hate was so great that not only was it corrupting me – ruining my view of the world until I believed it was only foul – but, to my surprise, by some mysterious alchemy, it was turning into love. I was beginning to love my thief, a man I barely knew, but whom I had trusted and even liked, and who had taken my savings, amongst many other crimes. At one low point I was phoning him every hour. I was impatient with everyone else because I was thinking of him all the time. I was waking up at night to think of him more, and when he did call, my heart leapt. I would retreat to a quiet room where I could hear every tone of his voice. I would, I even thought, go to his house and see him in his privacy. I would become his stalker.

Freud wrote that love involves the undervaluation of reality and the overvaluation of the desired object. While the correct valuation of a person is an odd, if not impossible idea, we might say Freud meant something like this: for various reasons, many of them masochistic, we become involved with others who cannot possibly give what we ask for; we can wait as long as we wish, but they do not have it, and one day, if we can bear to abandon our fantasy and see clearly, we might face reality straight on. We will then look elsewhere for fulfilment, to a place where our needs can, in fact, be satisfied.

At the beginning of this business, one of my agents, the man who had recommended Chandler, had told me how impressive Jeff had been at meetings. Clever and decisive, Chandler had satisfactorily done my agent's accounts, as well as those of my agent's family. Chandler was on top of things. He knew what he was doing. Everyone felt in good hands. But, by the end, when everything had gone wrong, the truth was that Chandler did not have anything. However, he remained confident and liked to give the impression he did have it all. Or he maintained that he would have it soon: funds were on their way from Spain or Switzerland. And so I kept asking for it, but he knew, and I realised eventually, that he had lost everything. It would never come back, and this was a loss I would have to live with, think about, and attempt to integrate.

*

Pop and the theatre, my first cultural loves, are both, in form and content, games of deception, deceit and mischief, where there is nothing authentic or real behind the artificial front, except the desire to play and to be someone else. David Bowie knew that pop was a put-on; he lifted and modified everything that interested him. I've always been fascinated by the nefarious cleverness of hypnotists, tricksters, card sharps, mountebanks, con men, convincers, deceivers, big-mouths, bigamists, hiders and cheats; men who had three families living in one neighbourhood unbeknownst to one another, others who pretended to be doctors, pilots or Olympic swimmers, or who concealed an evil past as a Nazi. I like to think of the man who tried to sell the Eiffel Tower to an industrialist by convincing him it was to be used for scrap metal. I think of undercover agents, of anyone who has talked someone into something, someone with nothing who can persuade others, using words, that they have it all, or at least something desirable. The con man is the one who has the password to your hopes, who touches the G-spot of your wishes. Honesty and straightforwardness are dull; the con man makes you aware that life could be more gratifying than it is. He is everyone's procurer, the sorcerer who conjures fantasy in you, the ever-flowing mother who will fill you up with good things, the one who can identify what you want even before you see it yourself. One shouldn't forget that Hans Christian Andersen's tale 'The Emperor's New Clothes' is the story of an almost successful con, of a couple of weavers who convince an Emperor that he is more than he is. His vanity is their instrument, and they play on him until he is exposed and humiliated.

As many of us do, I come from a family of show-offs, fantasists and big-mouths, and I wanted to be big myself, once – bigger than I in fact was. Sometimes I even believed we big-mouths were all in the same game: isn't a writer a kind of con artist or spell-binder, telling stories for their life like Scheherazade, drawing the other into a conspiracy of lies, convincing them to turn the page and believe in flapdoodle?

Naturally, I identified with the con man and his omnipotence over the other, and not with his victims. But in this case I was the victim; I was the seduced, taken one. Jeff Chandler had helped himself to my money, and he had robbed me of more than that: of an orienting and useful connection with reality, which, once it had slipped away, left me feeling bereft, abject, dizzy and out of control. He had done me over, and done me in.

Long before this, though, and long before I learned that the insane, these days, might disguise themselves as money experts, I had heard that no one had met a sane accountant. Certainly, one of my previous accountants had been unwashed, almost incoherent and, at the end, covered in paint smears, having fallen, he said, into a fence on the way to my place. Nevertheless, before this collapse he'd been a mixture of insanity, probity, cunning and high intelligence.

For my part, I was a good bourgeois bohemian who had always earned a reasonable and steady income. I considered my single duty was to support my children, otherwise I liked not having to think about money. As I needed an accountant, a kind friend then recommended someone competent they knew, but said she sidelined as a rubber-clad dominatrix at night. You could file your expenses and get a whipping. I thanked my friend, but thought that as the work was relatively simple, it might be a good idea to go with the straightest person I could find, a pillar of the community. And Jeff Chandler appeared to be upright. The firm he'd been a partner in for ten years – they'd been around for seventy – were the acme of respectability, with smart offices and a successful clientele. This lower-middle-class clerk would know and follow the rules, so that I could break them in my imagination. That was the idea. What could go wrong?

It was a relief when Jeff turned up at my place, appearing competent, unflustered and on top of it all. What one wants, sometimes, is certainty and a guide, someone who knows better than you what they are doing. Jeff didn't appear to be superinflated like some people. And I'd been trained, as a child, to be something of a truster; as a writer, I was a listener.

*

When the con man walked through my door for the first time, I saw a small, chubby fellow with a high voice whom I could imagine singing enthusiastically in a choir. He wore cheap brown shoes and a clammy suit, and he soon informed me that his hobby was collecting James Bond memorabilia. Alongside his love of thrillers, he managed the finances of several churches, running their fund-raising quiz nights. His Congregationalist church in Essex supported other, similar churches in Albania. This was how, apparently, he had met his Albanian 'fiancée', as he always described the woman he seemed to be involved with. Super-friendly, easy-going with an undogmatic nature, Jeff said I could call anytime. And, indeed, he wore his telephone headphones continuously, muttering away into the mouthpiece even as he walked into my house and sat at my table, waiting for me to fetch him some water. He was always available, he declared, except on Sunday morning, when I was not to ring since he was at church with his family. He was devout, and didn't drink alcohol; he'd never had a hot drink: even the madness of tea had never passed his lips.

He said he took over a hundred phone calls a day. Sometimes he worked for twenty-three hours straight. When busy, he slept only every other day. I thought: well, there's a lot of heroically manic madness about, and most of it is not virulent. Think how agitated fluidity and rushes of ideas can be harnessed, for instance, to art. I liked him; for a while I was fascinated and even envious. Why an artist would envy an accountant might seem a mystery. But doing nothing – a large helping of tedium and dreaming – is essential to a writer's activity. How wonderful to be like him, with such a quick brain, and so in demand. Having so much to do, playing with money so competently, the hours must fly by in a fuss of earthy materialism. In comparison, we artists are of no use at all until others make us so.

Artists are always ambiguous about themselves, and certainly about their position within society. Are we inside or outside? Does what we do have any social utility? Should it have? Are we in showbiz or in service? Just as the dream escapes the utilitarian agency and vigilance of the daily self, and disproves the belief that we can rule ourselves, most proper writers would rather be at what I call the 'Genet' end of the scale, with the criminals, thieves and 'bedlam boys', than situate themselves within the farce and falsity of respectability. Art comes from chaos to make more chaos. The artist escapes the constraint of what he has done before, when he can; he has to. And, every day, I had to struggle against the impulse to become more conventional, to regress to the easy. My fears had been keeping me too safe.

*

The second time Jeff came over he made his move. He told me that the company, as it stated on its website, made investments for its valued clients. Many of his friends, as well as long-term clients, including several other writers (whose names he was not allowed to provide), were investing in a scheme he was running on behalf of the accountancy firm. The idea was to raise two hundred thousand pounds for someone to use as proof of funds. All Jeff had to do was keep my money safely for a hundred and twenty days, before returning it with good interest. He knew I had broken up with my girlfriend, and then with another girlfriend, and had school fees to pay. I was no longer earning a great deal. It was going wrong, my day seemed to be done, and advances for books and films had fallen away for everyone. Interest rates had crashed, and people were losing their jobs. Beneath most of us there is an abyss, and sometimes your foot plunges into it, and you understand something about catastrophe and loss. Most of my contemporaries, the ones who hadn't become rich in the good times, were teaching. The academy had become our patron, as good a use for it as any: we supported the students, and the university bought us time to write.

The interest Jeff offered was high, but that was because it was only a short-term deal, he explained, and I was fortunate to get in on it so late on. More than a hundred and twenty days after my initial investment Chandler paid the interest owed. I left the capital with him, and offered him a larger chunk of money. Muttering into his phone as always, he drove me to the bank to pick it up, his feet barely touching the pedals of his huge 4x4, his computer parked securely on the dashboard.

If he seemed particularly panicky and agitated that day, I put it down to his frantic life. But, looking back, I can see that he knew, at the moment when I signed over the money to him, that he was deceiving me, that it was all a lie, and this money, which I had put aside for my children's education, would be lost. But he said nothing and just smiled. By then I'd given him more than a hundred thousand pounds, which was the money he never returned, the money he stole, either stashing it somewhere, or losing it to other scammers.

This, it turned out, was the least of it. During this period, in the spring of 2012, he and I were doing business in a building society not far from my house. Jeff was helping me to 'get more' from my accounts. He asked me to give him my driving licence, which was my ID, to show the assistant at the teller's window. He must have copied it, because a few days later my account at the building society was empty, having been raided. I didn't become aware of this for a couple of weeks, until I returned to the building society to take out some money and found that my account had been gutted. That moment was like being hit in the face with a brick; I sat down with my head in my hands for some time, attempting to arrange the fragments of this story into one piece. I learned, much later, after a lot of confusion, that Jeff had gone into a branch of the building society in North London, where I'd never been, shown some version of my ID, forged my signature and walked out with eighty thousand pounds.

The afternoon of the discovery, despite my shock, some instinct made me continue with my detective work. I went into the branches of several building societies near where I lived, asking if they had accounts in my name. The first two didn't, but it turned out that the third one did. When I enquired about this I had the uncanny experience of being asked by the branch manager if I was 'the real' Hanif Kureishi or an imposter. 'How do we know you're you,' he said, 'and not the other man?' 'I have ID,' I said. 'But he had ID,' he replied.

While I am someone who likes to entertain interesting questions, and never mind the fact the branch manager had become a philosopher of epistemology, I had been taken over. My name belonged to someone else. I had become a nobody, a cipher, while Jeff had turned into me. After ruminating on this vertiginous reversal, I said that an imposter wouldn't be this furious, and wouldn't shout. Surely he would be nervous. 'His signature is the same as yours.' He pushed a copy across the desk. It bore no resemblance to mine. How could I prove that two quite different things were two quite different things? The situation got worse when it turned out that Jeff had also given a false address in South London. I checked the location; it was very near my childhood home. I planned to go there and run into myself, living another life. We could be introduced.

But I hadn't thought this through yet, or even realised Jeff was involved; it hadn't occurred to me. So, after this crime was committed I rang the criminal immediately, knowing he would help me. And he did. Jeff was furious with the building society for handing out my money on a forged signature. He said if he had more time he'd go to the building society and tear a strip off them. It was obvious the signatures wouldn't match. It was like the Wild West out there, he said. There were at least ten thousand fraud attempts a day on British banks, and many of them succeeded. Fortunately, the building society took responsibility – having handed out my money rather easily – and returned the amount. It was a while, though, before I could think this through, and work out that it was Jeff himself who had deceived me, and then attempted to help. I should have gone with Miss Whiplash, the dominatrix.

Also during this period, when Jeff must have been very mad and busy, when the self which had perhaps dominated and contained him seemed to have been overrun by a more sinister invincible self – the whole of his energy and intelligence had become committed to extreme suicidal thievery – Jeff tried to persuade me to raise a mortgage on my house. This would release more funds for his 'investments'. Luckily I didn't proceed, because about a month before Jeff was due to return my capital and the next tranche of interest, I received a phone call from the accountants saying Jeff had been sacked. Another writer had noticed that money was missing from his account, and had warned the firm, who then investigated Jeff's computer. It turned out that Jeff had stolen from the firm in which he was a partner, as well as from numerous other friends, charities and clients whose money he had invested in various flimsy schemes. If I wanted to know what was going on, I should call him – and they gave me his number and email address, and put the phone down. That was the last word his partners said on the matter. Everyone else in the company he worked for denied all responsibility.

It occurred to me to call Jeff. He answered his phone and, as always, he was available and chatty. It was a relief that he hadn't disappeared and was willing to offer an explanation. That evening he came over to my local cafe and told me he'd got into difficulty with the investments. He didn't like the word 'steal', he said, as he'd never intended to keep the money for himself. He had 'moved' people's money about, as financial gaps began to appear around him. He had borrowed money from some clients to pay off others. As he explained this, he also spoke to other clients on his phone; on another phone he was on the internet, on eBay, where he was trying to sell his sofa, some artwork, other household items and, hardest of all, his James Bond toys. His hands were shaking, his voice was weak, he could barely speak.

In Gabriel García Márquez's great story 'There Are No Thieves in This Town' a feckless thief steals the billiard balls from the bar's only billiard table, which is, more or less, the only entertainment in the little flyblown town. As the tale unwraps, we see that this theft causes chaos; there is a tsunami of unintended and unpredictable consequences, of guilt, revenge and violence. By the end the thief is attempting to make reparation, but that also goes wrong. At one point he considers fleeing, as if attempting to get away from himself, so noxious has he become, but where could he go?

It was getting hot for Jeff, recriminations were piling up, and a few days later he fled. He went to Spain, either to hide out from the anger directed his way, or to try to retrieve some of the money which had been stolen from a joint bank account by a lawyer who turned out to be 'a scammer', despite the fact Jeff had had him checked out. It looked as though Jeff had believed he could make some money, but had fallen into a brood of vipers, a nest of crooks. Not that I should worry about anything, he said during one of his daily phone calls from Spain. One of his more trusting investors had given him some money to live on while he recovered the stolen stuff. He was, he told me, right now standing outside the house of the scammer who had stolen our money. He could see the bastard through the window. Jeff had followed and confronted the man when he went to his office. Now the man closed his curtains and didn't go out. Chandler was 'shutting him down'. Jeff had also, undercover, sent hard men to threaten various parties. Not that this Spanish investment was the only one he had going. There was another, in Switzerland, which would come through later. There was no doubt, he said, that the money would turn up. It was only a question of when. What was wrong with a little patience?

He began to call me regularly from Spain, sometimes twice a day. When I told him what anguish and shock this theft, this violation and stupidity, had visited upon me and my family, and when I wondered what the point of his promises was, he'd apologise for what he'd done, saying his only chance was to pay everyone back. There was no point in any of us contacting the police, he said; the money would never be returned if he was in prison. I had to give him one more chance; he knew how to sort it out. Crime hadn't been his career choice, otherwise he'd have disappeared to Albania, where his fiancée's family lived, and where he could, at least, have worked as an accountant. No; he'd made the wrong move because the scheme had looked good to him, and he'd invested for us. And for himself, of course. Still, all would be fine; my money would be returned 'by Thursday'. It became a family joke. He was the 'Thursday man'. Many Thursdays came and went, yet his little squeaky voice was always optimistic. The money would 'definitely' turn up. 'They have no choice,' he'd say. 'It's our money.' It was yes, yes, yes, with him. And so in this way days, weeks, months passed.

Not speaking to the police was the only leverage I had over him. But then he exhorted me to pity him. He had placed himself, I could see, at the centre of a large network of people who were dependent on him. Having obtained money from twenty of his friends, as well as members of his own family, all these distressed people were now calling him; they all required information, and he connected us all, sitting in the centre of the shattered mirror of his life, like a broken, helpless king muttering meaning-less phrases.

There was another thing. One morning, just before he left for Spain, Jeff had rung to say he hadn't been in contact because his mother's sister had died and he'd been at another funeral. Soon he informed me that two of his investors and three members of his family had recently died. His fiancée's mother was on the verge of death. They were dropping like flies; he seemed to be aware that he was killing everyone around him. We had entered a wild disorder – the realm of death, if not murder – in his mind. But not only had he stolen from me, and, in total, about four million pounds from others, he wanted consolation and support. He had it, too; I threw myself into an orgy of encouragement. What an unlucky fellow he was with everyone dying around him, and what a bad year he was having in this cemetery of ghosts. Was there anything I could do? If he ever needed to talk, I was there. When it occurred to me to go to his house and stand outside, watching his move-ments and seeing how he lived, I visualised relays of semi-concealed desperate voyeurs observing one another while attempting to remain unnoticed.

Once, later, when I couldn't find him, when his

phone was cut off in Spain because he couldn't pay the bill, I fell into a sort of raging madness, and didn't know what to do with myself. I walked, I punched things and shouted obscenities; at one point, I was phoning him every fifteen minutes. I just had to know where he was. But perhaps he was busy soothing the many others he had reduced to the same condition?

There was nothing sensuous or erotic in all this fury and despair. In fact, it could lead you to believe that life is hopeless, and nothing but a trap. Yet however ridiculous, shaming and humiliating it was, the game could not end. That was the one thing which could not happen. Jeff was the lover I always wanted to hear from and was even keener to see. I would beg him for a 'new lie', and he would give me one, and they were some of the best lies I'd ever heard. He was never haughty, cruel or taunting, but always straightforward, as if he understood that deception was a medicine I required urgently. Forever waiting for my man, I was reminded of a coke dealer I had in the nineties, a sweaty, paranoid madman whose eventual arrival in a knackered Rolls-Royce, with a pit bull – a snuffling violent ball of threat which he would release in my flat – was greeted by me as a great event, as the highlight of the day. I'd given Jeff my savings, why not give him my time and health and life too? Usually, when one believes one is most safe, one is in most danger. But I knew how easy it is to become addicted to catastrophes, and how difficult it is to let go of violent pleasures. What was happening to me?

There's a passage in Nietzsche's *The Gay Science* which states, 'What if a demon crept after you one day and said to you, "This life, as you live it now and have lived it, you will have to live again and again; and there will be nothing new in it, but every pain and every joy and every thought and sigh will have to return to you, all in the same succession and sequence. The eternal hourglass of existence is turned upside down again and again, and you with it, speck of dust."' And in *Thus Spake Zarathustra* Nietzsche writes, 'Time is a circle. Do you desire this innumerable times more?'

I began to wonder if I was being thrust back into something I recognised. I come from a South London suburb, and though Jeff was in his early forties and I'm fifteen years older than him, growing up in 1960s South London I knew plenty of post-war spivs and wide boys like him. The area was full of smart and nasty thieving crooks and off-the-back-of-a-lorry merchants. The other significant interest of the suburban young was music. A lot of bands made the relatively short journey to the suburbs, and many kids were starting to form groups. The music and the drug dealing and thieving had one thing in common, which was a kind of defiance of dead authority and the manufacture of excitement through transgression. But the music we heard and made, and the clothes and creativity which came out of it, was alive, and represented a future, while the thievery was a futility. But I couldn't, then, always tell them apart, and the mad thing was, I still hadn't learned.

*

Chandler told me the police arrested him on the plane when he came back from Spain. This annoyed and embarrassed him in front of the other passengers. 'I wasn't going to run away. They didn't need to do that,' he told me sniffily. Apparently he didn't say much when the police interviewed him, and he was soon on bail. Over Christmas we met a couple of times and he continued to say the money was about to turn up. He was not pleased with the police. They were not giving him the chance to retrieve the money, and they had upset his frail mother by mentioning jail. Couldn't they be more sensitive? I asked him how his Sundays were, how going to church with his family, in such circumstances, made him feel. He said it had been difficult for them all – there had been 'looks' – since it was now known that he had stolen the church fund he had been charged with taking care of. But he was keen to let me know that 'God is a forgiving fellow'.

'That's all right, then,' I said.

'Many of the others will never be repaid, but for you there is still a way out,' he said, leaning forward.

Unsurprisingly for someone so isolated and living in their own mind, there were labyrinths of mysterious complication without conclusion which he confused and bored me with. But it seemed to boil down to this: though he wanted to pay me back, since he'd been pinched by the police and couldn't move money around in his own name, I had to open an account in Nevada or the Channel Islands. That way the money wouldn't show up in my bank statements. Or I could, he said, go to Switzerland, pick up the money in cash, and carry it in a suitcase to another bank. I pictured myself walking around Geneva with thousands of euros in a bag, and while the idea made me laugh, I wondered how things had come to such a pass, and what my children would think. I told him I was ready to book my flight. I was keen to see Geneva, even in winter.

In the cafe that day, examining this peculiar little Lucifer in his cheap shoes, as his phones buzzed at his fingertips, a man who had just smugly announced he'd forgiven himself, I considered the enigma of madness. How could he appear so unworried? How could he deem a catastrophe and the creation of so much fury a local difficulty? I wanted to know him, but he did not want to know himself. Nothing about his own state of mind concerned him. Perhaps his actions were his only thoughts, and there was nothing in his mind at all. Not that distress did not exist. He had inserted it into us, his victims, rendering us afraid, depressed, furious, sleepless, guilty, while he was blithe and even jaunty. Not that such separation doesn't happen all the time. In this Hollywood world of heroes and villains, good and evil are kept apart; there is no confusion, ambiguity or subtlety. And when, at the end of the Hollywood piece, the two antitheses confront one another and fight to the death, good always succeeds. But when evil is a form of goodness, when, say, it is innocent or even altruistic, there occurs something which cannot be grasped, let's call it an impossibility. And it was this I was trying to know, and, eventually, write from or out of.

Jeff told me he was ringing his victims regularly, to calm them down and keep them informed, though one of his school friends, whom he persuaded to invest his savings, was about to lose his house. But still I wouldn't hear it when people I'd confided in dismissed Jeff as a toxic little thief. Jeff was a hero for wanting to make reparation; he was doing his best: he was aware he had almost run out of chances. If idiots are elevated into gods all the time, he was at least my idiot. Not only were we friends, I would continue to believe that he would deliver me into the light, and then I would be happy and free. Yet how is it that people can get stuck inside you, like dreams which refuse to yield up the secrets of their horror, and you can't wake up or grasp what's going on? I began to mirror his behaviour. Manically obsessed with him, I couldn't sleep. I wished him to die, but ended up wishing I could die.

*

As I walked about, thinking him through, it came back to me, after a while, where I had seen something like this before. Had Jeff always been there? In what sense had he – or a man resembling him – always been present in my life? And when I wasn't using him to undermine and depress me, what use could he be? Would I have to look at his face forever? For there were, when I could bear to think about it, an eternity of Jeffs, of mostly older men whose stories I'd attend to. There are friends you begin to hate even as you love them, even as they waste you, and you refuse to see how tiresome and what an expense it all is. What emerges in such friendships is the same thing repeatedly, until both partners become sadistic. The ending of significant friendships is painful, yet still I believe in the future; rebirths are possible: there are conversations where new things can be said and heard.

*

My father, born in Madras, had been at the younger end of a large family of mainly boys who were rough and competitive. In his early twenties my father came from Bombay to London to study and to make a new life. He married an Englishwoman, left college and settled in the suburbs, where the quiet and regularity suited him, and he liked the people. But Dad's job, in the Pakistani Embassy, was dull and badly paid, and without a pension. My mother and I urged him to find a better job and, at one point, he considered joining the police as a clerk. He also considered becoming a traffic warden. But in the end

Dad refused to change. He thought he was better than all that: another job was unimportant, it was nothing, because soon, he imagined, he'd become a writer. He would have the dignity and class an artist deserved. But until then we had to provide encouragement and support, keeping the faith. We were supposed to be fans and believers, maintaining the master in his place. Our love and confidence would keep him afloat, just as the prayers of the faithful keep God from discouragement. Whatever happened, we could never be disappointed in Dad; the good thing would turn up. After all, self-belief is necessary, isn't it? And, surely, one should have grit and never give up.

However, I figured out, years later, that I in particular had been persuaded. I had betrayed a more thoughtful and realistic position, getting everything the wrong way round. Somehow I had joined a protection racket or cult. Whatever happened, Dad couldn't be disenchanted, or taste the bitterness of failure. It had become my job, as his disciple and imitator, to shield him from truths which, however tough they might have been, could have made him more imaginative. That was my naivety; but I was young, and this was ages ago, before I could recognise how necessary and important disappointment is, and long before I saw that others' delusions keep them sane, but don't necessarily do the same for us.

*

In many other ways, my mates and cohorts and those a bit older in the sixties and seventies, mature property owners now, were a generation of hoodwinked fools. We, who had denounced and given up on numerous authorities, had sought new masters over and over again. Friends, and those in our circles, were Maoists, Stalinists and Trotskyites of various types; others I knew followed Scientology and similar groups, like EST (Erhard Seminars Training), to which they showed cult-like dedication. We doubters seem to be easily impressed by those with conviction. And it is the attitude of the believer rather than the belief itself which is the crucial thing here. Whether it's political or scientific salvation, seventy-two virgins waiting in heaven, a particular example of satanic ritual abuse, or the idea that one has a crucial message of liberation for the world, it is the state of absolute certainty and dogmatism which is the menace. The idea that by removing the object of the delusion one will cure the delusion is itself a delusion. Delusions are two-a-penny; what is significant is the attitude taken towards the material. Any fool can believe the sun will rise tomorrow: it takes a certain kind of absurd commitment to believe in, say, the efficacy of lifelong celibacy, or prayer or heaven, or some kind of political paradise – or to believe in a con man. It is the absurdity of the belief which makes the commitment to it absolutely necessary, and the intractability of the conviction will be in inverse proportion to the unsustainability of the idea.

In my case absurdity had certainly created commitment. I and some others kept Jeff going, as if he had started his own religion. But it was from this engagement with Jeff that a question formed in my mind, one of the most important there is. Can one person drive another person mad, persuading them to forsake that which is truly of value, collapsing their mind so they see reality askew? Certainly, adults can drive children mad, and adults can make one another crazy by creating conflicts in them which seem insoluble, or for which the only solution might appear to be a retreat into inner chaos and disintegration. Jeff seemed to have that effect on me. But if my head was parked under the bed, I had to wonder about my own part in putting it there. I seemed to have willingly joined a sect and come to believe that my suffering was worthwhile and would lead, eventually, to relief and happiness. I had believed Jeff was the solution when he was the problem, and that my madness was the only thing keeping me sane.

Sometimes you can only get anywhere by giving up on people, by cutting the links between you. How do you begin to do that? With Jeff, it felt as if he was no longer a real person in the world, but, rather, as if I'd swallowed but could not digest him. People can kill themselves to get rid of a devilish persecutor inside them.

*

The last time we met, in a cafe near my house, Jeff wasn't in good shape. His fiancée seemed to have disappeared, and she didn't want to know anything about where he'd got so much money from, or even hear from him again. Thugs had been coming to his place to threaten him, and he'd had to call the police. It seemed to me that his mania had surrendered to disintegration; his body had given up and he couldn't get out of bed or wake up properly. He could barely breathe or talk. I told him that it had been nine months since my money had gone missing, and I was going to give a statement to the police. He looked alarmed and promised to give me a 'little bit' on Monday, and he winked. To prove it – and, perhaps to keep up appearances – he showed me a bank statement for forty-three million rials belonging to a Dubai sheik he'd 'invested' for.

I laughed and attempted to add to the bitterness of his woes by telling him that I'd worked briefly in a women's prison and could still recall the hopeless cries of the self-harmers and the clink of keys being turned in locks. He nodded and said that it was now inevitable that he would have to do 'time'. He knew he wouldn't like it in jail, particularly as he was claustrophobic. His voice began to break, and he said he'd only stolen money – or 'borrowed' it, as he preferred to put it – when he'd received a notice claiming to deliver £350,000 to his account. He'd then begun to move money around, and everything went crazy, as it can when you get desperate and start to panic. I visualised him being encircled by those he'd wanted to enrich; and I knew he feared being shut in, and returned to the place he was most afraid of. The claustrophobic desires his own immurement, and he had brought it about that he would be shut in for a long time.

That's justice for you, and as I watched the sexless, bland bean counter walk away, it just seemed obvious that time is more valuable than money. If it

took me a while to see this. Chandler had done me
a terrible disservice by creating the impression that
money was the only important thing in the world,
that it was love itself, the milk of paradise, the medi
um that mattered the most, being more important
than ideas, or poetry, or friendship or conversation.
This was the point at which communism and capitalism met: where the single value was the crudest
form of social utility.

*

One day I was released – by the pitying look on a
good friend's face. After he'd heard me out for at
least the third time, he was firm. 'More than enough
already,' he said. 'This has gone too far. Let him go.'

'Has it gone too far? Are you sure?'

'All you can do is write it out.'

My heart sank, and my instinct was to resist such a
terrible truth, one which was disruptive and uncom-
fortably liberating, connecting me to that which
Henry James referred to as 'the grim face of reality'.
After all, the masochistic bond is one of the strongest there is. We choose our oppressors; we love them
like our parents. Doesn't La Boétie write somewhere,
'Freedom is the one thing which men have no desire
for'? I wandered around for a few days as if I'd been

punched. Eventually, I dragged myself to my desk. Perhaps my friend was correct; perhaps there was nothing else for it but the breaking of that bond of voluntary servitude, and serious reflection. Jeff had enlarged my fears, at times making them very large indeed. But at least I could see what they were. I had to find a way to live around them.

It is exhausting work to disperse all goodness and create futility and pointlessness. None of this wild fantasy had been good for Jeff, for me, for anyone. Artists have an imagination, their minds can go anywhere, but their feet have to be on the ground, and their words organised. Insofar as it was possible, I would have to see Jeff as he was, and consider what I'd made of him. It can be real work keeping alive the most important things, and everybody hides from that which matters most to them. When it comes to writing, it is probably true that human weakness in all its varieties is the only subject there is, and I had had more than enough of that.

I began to write, throwing down thoughts as they occurred to me, while not being sure as I began on this piece that writing is quite the cure it can be made out to be. Not only is writing an indirect and long-term form of communication, but doesn't writing open a wound before it heals it?

However: alone you cannot achieve anything; alone you can only return to where you were as a child. Writing is an adult transaction; there is always someone there, a real target, as it were, for your words, which should be open-ended and fresh. Words are the strongest material there is, and telling stories is a form of action which changes reality. My relationship with Jeff was not dead; it was worse than that, it had been actively destructive and still was, its only consolation and reward being a little perverse excitement and complicity. For me to try and find another way through this difficulty was to give up my addiction to the idea that he would deliver. Loss is the price of knowledge: I would have to forsake something comparatively easy for something more difficult, forfeiting the accelerations of love and hate for the relatively low mood of mere sadness and acceptance. Art, like the best conversation, re-frames conflicts, representing them in ways which enable fresh thought, generating more plausible stories. A third thing, something brand new, would eventually have to emerge from the stasis and despair of this filthy, stupid dialectic. After all, I wondered, who did my mind belong to – my father, my children, my accountant? How could I retrieve it? What agency did I have over it? It seemed to me, after all this, that having a peaceful, creative mind was a most desirable thing. The most fortunate people, it seemed, were those with least anxiety, and I was a long way from that.

The police had written to me about Jeff. While I'd been giving Jeff a chance to come up with the money, I hadn't replied. Now, after my hopes had run their vain course, I called them. They were well aware of Jeff, and had been gathering material and information. However, several victims hadn't been found or come forward. Some were too rich to notice or get embroiled. Many of these suckers were understandably embarrassed; they'd been greedy and seduced, and couldn't admit to themselves or their families what they had let Jeff do to them. Some believed they had insufficient evidence to prosecute him, and others were still helping Chandler, chained to the illusion, believing he would deliver, unable to give up on him.

In the early spring of 2013, about a year after Jeff had gone on his spree, a detective came to take a statement from me. The policeman had recently been to see Jeff, who lived in a grim bungalow out in semi-rural Essex, with his parents in a shabby place at the other end of the plot of land. The policeman called it a backward, churchy, semi-rural community, with

very little worth selling. Greed was always under-
standable, he said, but Chandler's behaviour was
inexplicable. This man was doing well; he had come
far for someone with his background. As a partner in
his accountancy firm, his already large income would
only increase. Why would he sabotage himself for a
relatively small amount of dodgy money?

The policeman said Jeff seemed naive. A lot of
people said that about him. He must have been
led on by the Albanian girl he called his fiancée,
and they had spent six or seven thousand pounds
in one weekend at the Westfield shopping centre.
Jeff had bought property in Albania, a hairdress-
ing salon, a bakery and a restaurant, and put them
in her name. Jeff had once been quick and smart,
and a lot of people had told him that. But there is
always a horizon to people's intelligence, and they
must bear that in mind, since it is their fate. But
Jeff, with his James Bond omnipotence, couldn't do
that. There were no limits in the con man's world,
and perhaps he had come to believe he could do just
anything, steal and steal, and yet feel free. However,
where there is no prohibition there is no meaning,
and nothing real is possible. You would, I suppose,
begin to feel megalomaniacal and unconnected. In
truth, Jeff was ultimately a self-deceiver, a seducer

who had seduced himself, and a taker who had also been taken.

When the truth was discovered, Jeff's colleagues and former friends, people who had worked with him for more than ten years, some of whom he had employed and many of whom he stole from, scattered and scurried away. Bewildered and devastated by his deception, by all they did not know, they denied any responsibility for this disaster. They had not noticed he was a madman. Hiding behind lawyers gives people a sort of agency, or symbolic power, but it also exposes how weak they are. They're like people wearing a fright mask, and when it is ripped off you see the awful human fear beneath.

What shocks about a crime, I noticed, is not only the violation of limits, but the new knowledge of how insubstantial those limits were in the first place. Why, then, is it a relief and a disappointment when it turns out that the authorities, those we leaned against and even believed in, are themselves – and always were – foolish, perverse and dishonest?

*

Far from being an exception, a good man who inexplicably went wrong, Jeff was a monster created by the accountancy firm he partly built. As the necessary excrescence of the system, he embodied the Thatcherite ideal perfectly. Lower middle class, religious, a family man, self-motivated and hard working, he loved money more than he loved himself; he was a chancer, a corrupted wide boy, a charming crook who not only rose to the top of his profession, but destroyed everything around him. In the end, of course, the manic swings and crashes of bipolar capitalism had taken him too, but at least I understood now that far from being a maverick, an exception, the con man, the thief and liar, the man with the over-the-top interest rate, was the money world's most representative figure. A lunatic at the centre of a corrupt, collapsing system, like the 'mad' child in a family, he was its essence, the symptom that spoke its truth.

This view might be right. But it might not be. It is a good, convincing story, and anyone would rightly be suspicious of such cohesion and all that it excludes. So, such a narrative is probably irrelevant. But I couldn't stop thinking about Jeff and what sort of person he might be. Because he was no Machiavelli, plotting for advantage, power or wealth; he wasn't focused, predictable or readable. It must be odd to have nothing about you that is true, so I wanted to know what it would be like to be false through and through, a man you could look at and see nothing. I had, eventually, spoken to friends in the press about this story and some of it had become public, though the behaviour of Jeff's partners in the company had become disconcerting. However, I stuck to this thought: my money might have been stolen, but my words couldn't be. Yet even after this, and after he'd been arrested but not charged, I heard that Jeff was still peddling investments and spinning stories, a mad novelist, and a far-out magic realist at that, who couldn't stop making it up. I tried to get in touch with him, to ask him what he thought he was doing. He wouldn't answer. Jeff was not a great Dostoevskian criminal or poet of destruction, he was not truly selfish or savage when it came to the violation of limits. There was no additional liberty in his impotent transgressions; the rules were still in place. What he did was a form of random evil in its most banal sense, but he did become good at it, successfully causing despair, hopelessness and ruin. Not everyone can bear to do that; not everyone would want to face the consequences, to reap such hatred. But Jeff lacked imagination, taking no one anywhere. He was a destructive monster, and he was nothing of interest.

*

Though a lot of people lost important things, this was only a minor tragedy. But it made people who heard about it nervous. They saw that anyone could be found out and taken, however defended they might be, because everyone is dependent on someone else, and there is always something unknowable about others. However, I was duped by a con man but learned more about women than I'd known before. Women were outraged by the wrongness; the women came through, and taught me to depend on them. You can be direct with a woman and she will appreciate it. The women rang the appropriate people; they wrote letters, they talked to one another, and knew what to do. They blamed the right people.

It is no surprise that we are all spellbound by crime and criminality. As children we are continuously taught right and wrong and morality; we are exhorted to obedience and are tempted by defiance. We are told that if we behave well we will be rewarded, but we soon notice that these rewards mostly benefit the authority rather than us. At the same time, we sexualise disobedience and never abandon its dangerous compulsions. This makes it more difficult, rather than easier, to be free. For adults, most of television, cinema, the newspapers and fiction is concerned with detectives, offenders and punishment. And for good reason. This is where we think about whether we should be good or not, and what the cost of crossing the line is, and what the – usually higher – cost of renunciation is. This is where we think about the relation between pleasure and happiness, and between pleasure and its price. After all, most authorities are experts in denial. Where might we learn what pleasure really is, and who will teach us?

*

Jeff's fiancée, or his desire for her, might have been the detonator, but Jeff himself had become a little suicide bomb, devastating everyone around him. It turned out that Jeff stole from his friends – people he'd known since he was eleven – from the church his parents attended, from charities, writers, pension funds, and of course from his partners at the company he had helped build. The line he gave the victims, and the stories he told, his circuitous explanations, as the whole thing broke down were all the same. Painful conflicts between friends and colleagues broke out after Jeff's crimes. People argued, let one another down, and fell out. I yelled at people until I had to lie down. Jeff taught me, I guess, the necessity of boldness and exactitude in speech. Where before I'd been evasive and vague, I had to learn to be precise, and ask for what I needed. Then, once this story came out in the press, many people wrote to me and to each other. Some could only get in contact anonymously, and many chose to be ashamed. People believed that because they had fantasised about becoming richer they had actively collaborated in their own downfall. It was as if, for this minor crime of greed, each person had been seduced, fucked, fucked over, and discarded. However, some of the victims continued to defend Jeff, calling him 'innocent' or 'naive'. Of course, it was this facade of naivety which made him so dangerous and convincing. But there was also a part of him which was genuinely naive. It might have been the case that his sexual inexperience had made him hazardous, because he hadn't understood what was happening to him when he met the Albanian woman. He thought he had to impress her. Or give her everything. I remember now that the first time I met him he opened his wallet in order to show me a photograph of the woman he called his fiancée. The picture was indistinct but I could see that it was, at least, a woman. This action seemed an incongruous, old-fashioned thing to do. I thought he was showing me that the successful man is one who is loved. Now

I know it was the wallet, not the woman, he wanted me to see.

*

Thieves of time, thieves of friendship, affection and sexuality, thieves of your soul, stealers of dreams: bad loves, and even worse loves. The obscene, perverse, sadomasochistic death dance, both partners locked together in limbo. You could call these anti-loves. People love their suffering, and most thefts are even welcomed, as you can barely wait to give away that which is most valuable; and there are many thefts you don't notice because you are paying attention to the wrong things. When you do see at last, it can be a shock. Twilight: time is running down; there has to be an attempt at reparation – a release, if not a rebirth, converting action into thought and renewed creativity, into a better madness. Ruthlessness, particularly with oneself, is an art.

I know I'm ready for something fresh when I want to buy new notebooks. With scores of new pages to fill and flip through in anticipation, I can begin to believe I'm a writer again, the void of the empty page being an invitation and a limit to the disorder of my ideas.

My talent, such as it is, had not yet deserted me.

Whether I was distracted or not, I could write; I liked to write and worked longer hours than before. I like to wake up in the morning with the whole day ahead of me, in which I can write uninterruptedly. My writing was developing and changing, even if other things were getting worse by staying the same. I began to scribble these notes, and wonder about what sort of thief an artist is. Things had got too predictable in my life, and unpredictability – at least in the head – is the engine of creativity. I knew that I needed more imagination here. To be liberated from someone is to no longer have the enervating burden of thinking of them: that is one lesson that love can teach. How long had it been since I'd gone a day without this fool flailing in my mind? He had made me into someone I didn't like, and for a time I hated to wake up to myself. Jeff had taken my money, but what else had he taken? He had come far, according to the policeman, but I had come further, and would go much further. To be happy, I had to forget, and that is difficult.

I thought: I should steal from him. If I stole something back from this devil and homunculus, I could transform and remake him, pinning him to the page. If my despair had made me wonder what art might be for, I could at least now see that art is a glorious binding Eros, making new unities. Art might seem mad at times, but it has boundaries and structure; it has to. Where there was nothing there would be something new, a moment of light, an upsurge, invention. As an artist you have to force yourself to turn and look at the world, and the world is always worse, and more interesting, than you can imagine or render.